ETHAN FROME

by
Edith Wharton

Student Packet

Written by
Gloria Levine, M.A.

Contains masters for:

	1	Prereading Activity
	1	Study Guide (five pages)
	4	Vocabulary Activities
	3	Critical Thinking Activities
	5	Writing Activities
	2	Literary Analysis Activities
	1	Language Study Activity
	1	Review Crossword
	2	Comprehension Quizzes (two levels)
	2	Unit Exams (two levels)
PLUS		Detailed Answer Key

Note

The text used to prepare this guide was the Signet Classic softcover published by The Penguin Group. It was first published in English in 1911. The page references may differ in the hardcover or other paperback editions.

Please note: Please assess the appropriateness of this book for the age level and maturity of your students prior to reading and discussing it with your class.

ISBN 1-56137-513-6

Name________________________________

Directions: Rate each of the following statements before you read the novel. Compare your ratings with a partner's, and discuss why you chose the particular ratings you did. After you have completed the novel, rate the statements again.

1—— 2——3—— 4—— 5—— 6
agree strongly — *disagree strongly*

	Statement	Before	After
1.	Opposites attract.	_____	_____
2.	It is far better to endure unhappiness than to commit an action that brings public condemnation.	_____	_____
3.	Remorse is the poison of life, so never do something you might regret later.	_____	_____
4.	It is better to have loved and lost than never to have loved at all.	_____	_____
5.	Friends always forget those whom fortune forsakes.	_____	_____
6.	When two people get married, they shouldn't keep any secrets from each other.	_____	_____
7.	People shouldn't marry unless they are in love.	_____	_____
8.	A man has no excuse for cheating on his wife.	_____	_____
9.	People change.	_____	_____
10.	You shouldn't worry about what other people think.	_____	_____
11.	New Englanders are colder and more tight-lipped than people from other parts of the country.	_____	_____
12.	True love eventually wins out.	_____	_____
13.	Love doesn't last.	_____	_____
14.	Love is never having to say you're sorry.	_____	_____
15.	Families should take care of their own.	_____	_____
16.	The ends justify the means.	_____	_____
17.	Hypochondriacs are usually lonely people.	_____	_____
18.	Nasty people are usually unhappy ones.	_____	_____

Name______________________________

Directions: Write a brief answer to each study question as you read the novel at home or in class. Use the questions for review before group discussions and before your final test. Starred questions have no "right" or "wrong" answers.

* = thought or opinion question
** = prediction

Narrator's Introductory Comments

1. Why does Ethan's appearance make the narrator curious?
2. What happened to Ethan 24 years earlier?
3. Why didn't Ethan leave Starkfield?
4. Why is the narrator in Starkfield?
5. What did the narrator hire Ethan Frome to do?
6. Has Ethan ever left Starkfield?
7. What happens to the narrator's science book?
8. Why does Ethan invite the narrator to stay the night?

* 9. Does this beginning—a narrator trying to piece a story together from what different people have told him—remind you of any other stories you have read, or movies you have seen?

** 10. **Prediction:** What sort of "smash-up" did Ethan Frome have, 24 years earlier?

Chapter 1

1. Why didn't Ethan finish his college studies?
2. Why has Ethan come to the church at night?
3. Who is Denis Eady?
4. Why has Mattie been living in the Frome's house?
5. What does Ethan like about Mattie?
6. What does Zeena think of Mattie's housekeeping?
7. What reason does Zeena give for hiring another girl?
8. Why does Zeena mention that Ethan shaves every morning?

* 9. How do you think Zeena really feels about Mattie?

** 10. **Prediction:** Will Mattie Silver announce that she is getting married soon?

Name________________________________

Chapter 2

1. Who offers Mattie a ride?
2. How does Mattie tease Denis Eady?
3. What does Mattie tell Ethan about Ruth and Ned?
4. Does Mattie plan to leave the farm to get married?
5. How does Ethan "talk big" to Mattie?
6. What does Ethan think when he passes the graves?
7. Why are Mattie and Ethan surprised when they get to the door?
8. Why is Zeena still up when Ethan and Mattie get home?

* 9. Why do you think Edith Wharton includes this and other references to the graves of Ethan's ancestors?

** 10. **Prediction:** How will Zeena treat Mattie the next morning?

Chapter 3

1. What does Zeena say to Ethan once they are alone in the bedroom?
2. How has Mattie changed since she came to Starkfield?
3. What happened to Mattie's father?
4. Why did Mattie come to Starkfield?
5. Where is Zeena going?
6. How old are Ethan and Zeena?
7. Why does Ethan tell Zeena he has to collect cash for the lumber?
8. Why does Ethan regret telling Zeena he has to collect cash for the lumber?

* 9. How do you feel about Zeena?

** 10. **Prediction:** What do you think will happen now that Mattie and Ethan are alone together?

Chapter 4

1. How has Ethan changed since his college days?
2. What happened to Ethan's mother?
3. Why did Ethan marry Zeena?
4. Why wasn't Zeena willing to move out of Starkfield?
5. How did Zeena change after her marriage?
6. Why does Ethan ask Andrew Hale for an advance on his load?
7. What is Ethan afraid he will discover in the barn?
8. How does the pickle dish get broken?

* 9. What does Frome's attitude toward Starkfield seem to be? Is it a place where you would like to live?

** 10. **Prediction:** Will Ethan keep Zeena from finding out about the broken dish? If so, how? If not, how will Zeena react when she finds out?

Chapter 5

1. How do Mattie and Ethan spend the evening?
2. Why don't Mattie and Ethan go sledding?
3. Who did Ethan see kissing under the Varnum spruces?
4. How does the cat remind Ethan and Mattie of Zeena?
5. What does Ethan kiss?
6. What "nightly duties" does Mattie perform?

* 7. Why do you suppose Ethan doesn't kiss Mattie?

** 8. **Prediction:** When will Zeena return? How will she act?

Chapter 6

1. What is the weather like?
2. Why does Ethan plan to hurry to the village?
3. What job do Ethan and Jotham end up doing all day?
4. How does Ethan find some glue?
5. Why doesn't Ethan glue the pickle dish?
6. How does Zeena act when she gets home?

Name______________________________

7. Why doesn't Jotham accept Ethan's invitation to dinner?
8. How is this night like the night before?
* 9. Do you think Jotham and others are aware of how Ethan feels about Mattie?
** 10. **Prediction:** What will Zeena say about her trip to the doctor?

Chapter 7

1. What has the new doctor told Zeena?
2. Why has Zeena arranged for a "new girl" to come?
3. Why do Zeena and Ethan begin arguing?
4. Zeena catches Ethan in what lie?
5. Why does Ethan feel that he can't insist that Mattie stay?
6. Why does Ethan worry about Mattie's future?
7. Cite one example of Zeena's giving Mattie a "put down."
8. How does Zeena find out what happened to the pickle dish?
* 9. Why do you think Zeena was so angry about the pickle dish? Do you think she would have been as angry if Ethan had accidentally broken it while—say—fixing the cabinet?
** 10. **Prediction:** Will Ethan let Zeena have her way? Will Mattie be forced to go?

Chapter 8

1. Ethan has a room of his own. Describe it.
2. What message does Mattie leave for Ethan?
3. How did a man Ethan knows escape a similar life of misery?
4. What does Ethan write in a letter to Zeena?
5. What does Ethan see in the newspaper to upset him?
6. Why doesn't Ethan give the letter to Zeena?
7. What things does Zeena "go over" with Mattie?
8. Why does Ethan go to the Hales' home?
* 9. Do you think it is a sense of honor that keeps Ethan from asking the Hales for money—or is it something else?
** 10. **Prediction:** Will Ethan find a way to afford the trip out west with Mattie?

Name________________________________

Chapter 9

1. Describe how Mattie decorated her room.
2. Why does the blood rush to Ethan's face when Zeena tells him Mattie is getting down her trunk? (page 106)
3. What is the reason Zeena gives for wanting Jotham to drive Mattie to the station?
4. Why does Ethan drive the sleigh by Shadow Pond?
5. What plans does Mattie have for the future?
6. What does Mattie tear up? Why?
7. Why do Mattie and Ethan go down the hill on the sled the first time?
8. Why do Mattie and Ethan go down the hill on the sled the second time?

* 9. Why do you think Zeena doesn't say good-bye to Mattie? Does she feel at all ashamed?

** 10. **Prediction:** What happens to Mattie after the accident?

Narrator's Concluding Comments

1. How does Mattie look 24 years after the accident?
2. How do Mattie and Zeena get along now?
3. What does Mrs. Hale reveal about what happened after the accident?
4. How has Zeena changed since the accident?
5. How has Mattie's personality changed since the accident?
6. Why does Mrs. Hale say that it's a pity Mattie lived?

* 7. Do you think Ethan would have been better off if Mattie had died? if he had run off with Mattie? if he had put his foot down and refused to let her go?

* 8. Do you think the narrator's relationship with Ethan changes after spending the night at his home?

* 9. How do you think Mattie and Zeena treat the narrator?

* 10. Why do you think the narrator is so intrigued by Ethan Frome and his family? How much of the story do you think is "true"? Do you think Ethan Frome in his earlier years was what the narrator imagines him to have been?

** 11. **Prediction:** What do you think the Frome household will be like in 20 years?

Name________________________________

mien 4	taciturnity 4	sardonically 6	degenerate 6
capitulating 7	beleaguered 7	portico 8	wan 8
innocuous 8	reticent 8	livery 9	arid 10
sentient 11	inertia 13	plaintive 15	wraith 15
deciduous 15	reticence 16	querulously 18	droning 18
peristyle 20	tenuous 21	effrontery 23	fatuity 26
latent 27	dormant 27	intangible 27	incisively 29

Directions: The SAT and PSAT include 19 analogies. This exercise will give you practice with analogies. An analogy is a comparison. For example:

NO is to YES as OFF is to ON
HILL is to MOUNTAIN as STREAM is to RIVER

Use words from the vocabulary box to complete the analogies, below. Then create two of your own for a partner to solve.

1. WALLED is to STONEWORK as ______________________ is to ARMY.
2. CHUTZPAH is to TIMIDITY as ______________________ is to DIFFIDENCE.
3. BABBLING is to HUSHED as GARRULOUSNESS is to ______________.
4. MOVEMENT is to CHANGE as ______________________ is to STAGNATION.
5. ASLEEP is to AWAKE as ______________________ is to ACTIVE.
6. JOYFUL is to LAUGHTER as ______________________ is to TEARS.
7. WHOOP is to EXUBERANTLY as WHINE is to ______________________.
8. COURAGE is to HERO as ______________________ is to FOOL.
9. DOGS are to KENNEL as HORSES are to ______________________.
10. AFFABLY is to CORDIALLY as SARCASTICALLY is to ______________.
11. ____________ is to ____________ as ____________ is to ____________.
12. ____________ is to ____________ as ____________ is to ____________.

Name_______________________________

Directions: The SAT and PSAT include 19 sentence completions. This exercise will give you practice with sentence completions. Complete the sentence by picking the word that best fits into the blank.

1. She enjoys the display of _______________ and never fails to wear some piece of expensive jewelry.
   (A) volubility (B) stenography (C) imprudence (D) sociability (E) opulence

2. As the tide came in, the rowboat's gentle ___________ put the fisherman to sleep.
   (A) undulations (B) forebodings (C) pretexts (D) retorts (E) harbingers

3. The former athlete has a(n) ______ lifestyle now, and has put on several extra pounds.
   (A) suffused (B) scintillating (C) perceptible (D) sedentary (E) audible

4. Try as she will, she can't seem to buy enough groceries; her teenagers have _______________ appetites.
   (A) grotesque (B) irresolute (C) disdainful (D) fugitive (E) insatiable

5. Their annual family reunion is always a(n)_______________ gathering.
   (A) incredulous (B) convivial (C) ingenious (D) indentured (E) obstinate

6. They paused a moment in the darkened theatre to let their eyes adjust to the _______________.
   (A) inflection (B) obscurity (C) prolongation (D) merino (E) precedent

7. He usually enjoyed chatting and laughing with his friends on the way to school, but this morning he was in no mood for idle _______________
   (A) floundering (B) transplantation (C) capitulation (D) banter (E) allusion

8. She put a few items of clothing in the battered _______ and headed for the train.
   (A) knoll (B) counterpane (C) valise (D) gale (E) pot-pourri

9. The injuries she sustained in the accident _______ the athletic career she had planned.
   (A) preclude (B) discern (C) commemorate (D) obtrude (E) excel

10. He ____________ her not to drive after drinking, but she refused to listen.
    (A) barricaded (B) conjoined (C) spangled (D) implored (E) deplored

Name________________________________

Antonym Box

indolent 65	irrationally 73	sledge 74	derision 75
ineffectual 76	perfunctory 77	ponderous 77	ominous 78
stolid 78	stoicism 78	consecrated 80	felicitous 80
irretrievable 83	recrimination 83	rupture 86	pauper 86
antipathy 87	compunction 89	inexorable 90	regaled 91
affability 92			

Directions: Look in the antonym box for the word that means the opposite of the given word or phrase.

_____________ 1. rich person

_____________ 2. no regret

_____________ 3. alterable

_____________ 4. energetic

_____________ 5. light-footed

_____________ 6. auspicious

_____________ 7. thorough

_____________ 8. impatience

_____________ 9. productive

_____________ 10. continuity

_____________ 11. recoverable

_____________ 12. denied

_____________ 13. good-will

_____________ 14. praise

_____________ 15. logically

Name________________________________

Synonym Box

sequel 95	alimony 98	injunction 101	reflectively 102
ebullition 103	pretenses 105	wavered 106	monotonous 110
facetious 113	discursively 118	subdue 118	passively 118
contemptuously 119	exaltation 120	avowal 122	constrained 122
opaque 127	swarthy 127	immobility 128	relic 128
niche 128	tentatively 130		

Directions: For each of the words listed below, find a synonym in the synonym box. Write it on the line.

1. ____________________ dusky
2. ____________________ paralysis
3. ____________________ seething
4. ____________________ declaration
5. ____________________ meditatively
6. ____________________ frivolous
7. ____________________ ramblingly
8. ____________________ remnant
9. ____________________ docilely
10. ____________________ command
11. ____________________ inhibit
12. ____________________ scornfully
13. ____________________ recessed space
14. ____________________ not transparent
15. ____________________ tedious

Name_______________________________

Directions: With a partner, discuss Ethan's decision—before the accident—not to leave Zeena. What reasons did he have for wanting to leave her? What reasons did he have for staying? Were there any possible reasons the narrator didn't mention?

Take turns jotting reasons why Ethan should leave (in the YES Column) and should not leave (in the NO column). It is okay to write down key words and phrases rather than whole sentences. Try to include as many reasons under "YES" as you do under "NO." Discuss your charts with another pair of partners and try to reach consensus (agreement) on whether or not Ethan made the best decision. A spokesperson for this group of four should then report the group's conclusion to the whole class. Dissenting views of other groups should be heard at this time.

Yes	**No**
______________________	______________________
______________________	______________________
______________________	______________________
______________________	______________________
______________________	______________________
______________________	______________________
______________________	______________________

CONCLUSION:

☐ YES ☐ NO

On a separate sheet of paper, write an essay in which you explain and evaluate Ethan's decision to stay with Zeena. Provide specific reasons for why you do or do not agree that Ethan did the right thing.

Name______________________________

Directions: Two steps in problem solving are: (a) brainstorming possible solutions and (b) measuring each against specific criteria. When Mattie proposes that they sled down the hill "so't we'll never come up any more," Ethan faces a problem. Should he attempt suicide with Mattie? Help Ethan solve his problem by:

a) listing his choices in the chart below (those listed on the chart as well as others you can think of and add to the chart in boxes 4, 5, and 6)
b) listing criteria ("yardstick" questions used to measure how a particular decision "measures up" and what its effects will be), and
c) scoring each decision: 1=yes, 2=maybe, or 3=no.

	Criteria			
Possible Choices	Will our secret be safe?	Will anyone get hurt?	Will the world be a better place?	Will this create new problems?
1. Try to hit the tree.				
2. Tell Mattie it would be wrong.				
3. Get a divorce.				
4.				
5.				
6.				

Name_______________________________

Assignment: Write an essay comparing Zeena and Mattie.

Pre-Writing: In small group, complete the Venn diagram by listing words and phrases that describe each character below that character's name. Descriptive words that apply to both Zeena and Mattie should go in the overlapping area.

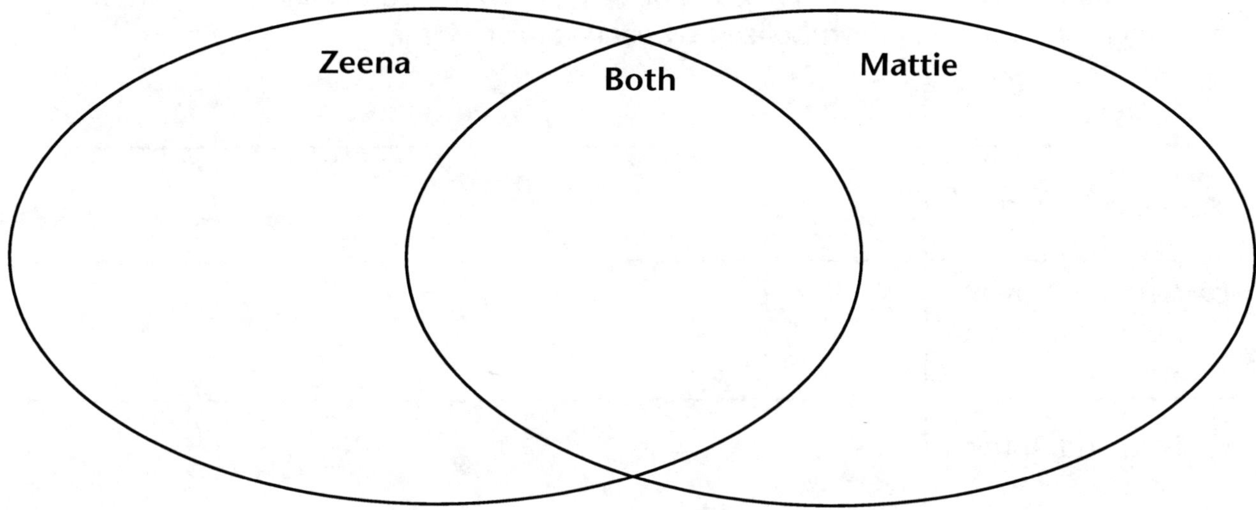

Mid-Writing: On your own, write an essay in which you compare and contrast the characters of Zeena and Mattie. Use some of the following transitional phrases to connect your ideas:

also, alike, both, common, equally, in the same way, just as/so, likewise, same, too, similar, similarly, although, but differ, different, however, in contrast, on the other hand, unlike, whereas, while

Incorporate details from the diagram to develop and support your statements about each character.

Post-Writing: Share your essay with members of your group. Ask for comments, particularly on focus (whether you adhered to the topic) and support (whether you provided enough reasons and examples in support of your statements).

Name______________________________

I. RESONANCE

Edith Wharton weaves a web of associations by repeating and varying certain words and actions. The echoes enrich the moods, human relationships, and symbolism in the story.

Find at least two references to each of the following and explain briefly what idea is emphasized or symbolized by each repeated image.

Image	Pages	Symbolizes
A. the color red		
B. sledding down below Varnum's spruces		
C. Ned and Ruth's kiss		
D. threshold		
E. snow		
F. the train		
G. Starkfield		

II. SETTING

Setting is the "time and place" of a story. It includes the physical background, the social settings, and the historical backdrop against which the story is told.

A. In approximately what year did Mattie come to the Frome farm? What clues help you estimate the year?

B. Where does the story take place? Briefly describe what the town looks like. Why did Ethan want to leave this place when he first married Zeena? Why didn't he leave?

Name________________________________

C. In what season does the story take place? How does the weather parallel Ethan's internal state?

D. List two references in the story to "recent" innovations in technology.

E. How does Mattie's room contrast with the rest of the house? What does this show about Mattie?

F. How does Ethan's room contrast with the rest of the house? What does this show about Ethan?

G. How has the interior of the Frome farm house changed after 24 years have passed? How does this reflect changes in Ethan?

III. DOPPELGANGER

A doppelganger (literally, "doublewalker") is a ghostly double or counterpart of a living person. It is a device with which Edith Wharton experimented.

A. Cite a detail describing Ethan's vision of Mattie as Zeena's ghostly double.

B. At the end, how do Zeena and Mattie look alike? act alike?

C. How is the narrator like Ethan Frome?

D. Why do you think Wharton has created these similarities? What is she trying to say about actuality and potentiality?

Name________________________________

Directions: Reread the section describing the sledding accident. Using the text and your imagination, record the answers to the questions on the Herringbone form below. (Who was involved? What did these persons do? When did it happen? Where did it happen? How did it happen? Why did it happen?) Add spaces if there are more than two answers to a question. Then write the newspaper article that appeared in the *Bettsbridge Eagle* the day after the accident.

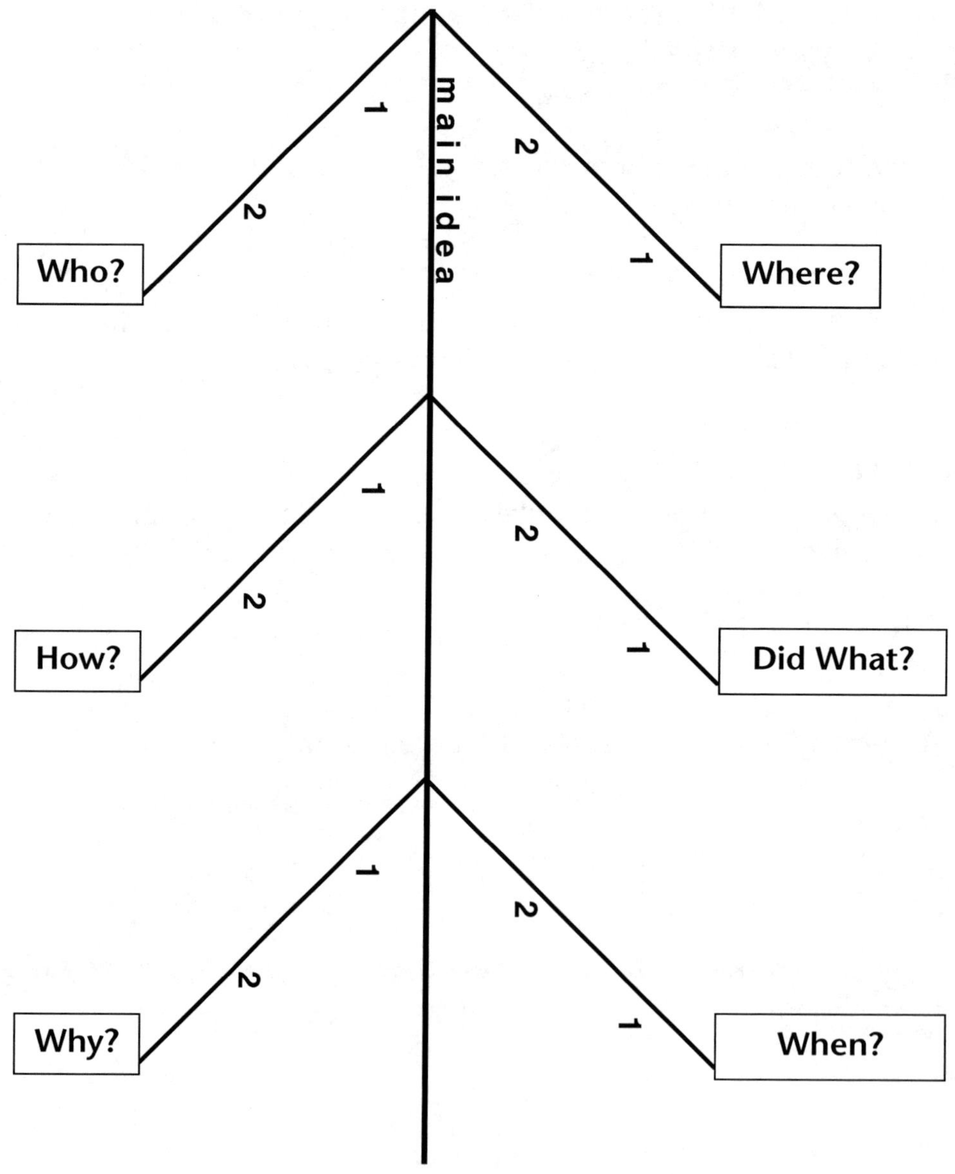

Name______________________________

Dialect: When the speech of two persons both speaking the same language exhibits marked differences in pronunciation, grammar, and/or vocabulary, they are said to speak different **dialects** of the language. Three broad areas of dialect are recognizable in the U.S.: "Eastern" (New England and Eastern New York), "Southern," and "General American" (or "Western"). Edith Wharton had a keen ear for dialect.

Directions: "Translate" each of the passages below into "standard English."

1. "There warn't ever anybody but Ethan. Fust his father—then his mother—then his wife." (page 5)

2. "We're kinder side-tracked here now...but there was considerable passing before the railroad was carried through to the Flats." (page 16)

3. "The doctor don't want I should be left without anybody to do for me." (page 28)

4. "...sometimes I can see she ain't suited, and yet I don't know why." (page 37)

5. "You... took the thing I set most store by of anything I've got..." (page 94)

6. "Oh, Matt, I thought we'd fetched it..." (page 126)

Name______________________________

Directions: Suppose that you are Zeena. You decide to write to "Gabby"—a syndicated advice columnist—using a disguised name and address.

Part I: Finish the letter below:

Dear Gabby,
I have been reading your column for years, and never cease to be amazed at how people air their linen in public. I never thought I'd be one of them, but here goes... I'm a thirty-something farmwife with a mountain of problems. First there's my husband— ____
____
____
____

Then there's my cousin's girl. I made the mistake of taking her in a year ago because
____
____
and now she ____
____

Finally, there's my health. I wore it down by ______________________
______________________________ and now ___________________
____

—Xenophobia in Bleakfield

Part II. In a small group, brainstorm various pieces of advice that Gabby might give "Xenophobia." Then write the letter that appears as an answer in her column.

Dear Xenophobia:
____
____
____
____
____
____
____

—Gabby

Name________________________________

In the novel, we see how Ethan reacts in the first moments of shock after the accident—but we do not know how he reacts a few days later. In this exercise, you will write a monologue for Ethan Frome that reveals what he thinks and feels when the reality of what has happened has set in.

Pre-Writing Listening Exercise:

(This part should be read aloud by a teacher or group leader.)

"Take a few minutes to relax and imagine the events of the past day or so. Recreate the scene where Ethan finds Mattie in the study, before heading to the train station. What do you see as you look around the study? What is the lighting like? What is Mattie doing? What does Ethan say to her? Can you see her wavering smile?...Now follow them outside to the sleigh. What does it look like? Do you see Ethan put Mattie's bag into the sleigh and tuck the rug around her? What expression is on both of their faces now?...Now watch as they head up the Bettsbridge road. Do you hear the conversation between Mattie and Ethan? Why are they stopping by the pond?...Now follow them as they get out of the sleigh. What are they saying about the picnic and the locket? Do you hear Ethan tell Mattie she is "as pretty as a picture" in her pink hat? Can you feel the cold, crisp air?...Now follow them back to the sleigh as they drive off. Can you see the sunset? Listen to what they're saying...Follow along as they approach the end of the village. Hear the sounds of the boys sledding near the church...Go with them as Ethan draws Mattie after him, toward the sled under the spruces...What are they saying? How are they feeling?...Follow them the first time they go down the hill...and the second time...Experience with them those final moments before the tremendous impact...Now put yourself in Ethan's shoes...What is that noise? You see Mattie...What are you thinking? ...Who comes to help you? Where are you taken? How do you feel?...How do you spend the next few days?...What memories pass through your mind? What are your thoughts about the future?...Now return to the here and now, pick up your pen, and take a few minutes to make some notes about what you have just seen, heard, felt, and thought about."

Assignments:

1. Do an oral improvisation of the scene. Speak your thoughts aloud, as in a stage soliloquy. You might find it helpful to tape the improvisation and play it back for discussion.
2. Transcribe your improvisation onto paper. As you write, think about Ethan's way of thinking, his speech patterns, his feelings toward Mattie, and the way he has acted in the past when upset.
3. Perform the monologue, complete with gestures, for others who have read the novel. Have them comment on how believable your monologue sounds. Are the thoughts themselves—and the words which you have chosen to convey them—consistent with Ethan as we know him in the novel? Is that the way you would expect Ethan to sound?

Name______________________________

Directions: A simile is a comparison which uses the words "like" or "as." Example: ***Her lips are like a red, red rose.***

Below are several similes found in Ethan Frome. For each one:

a) Tell what two items are being compared and how they are alike.

b) Create your own simile to express the same quality.

1. ...a lameness checking each step like the jerk of a chain. (page 3)

   a. ______________________ is like _________________________ because both

   ____

   b. ...a lameness checking each step like _________________________________

2. ...his profile...like the bronze image of a hero (page 11)

   a. ______________________ is like _________________________ because both

   ____

   b. ...his profile...like____

3. ...the musicians...belabored their instruments like jockeys (page 23)

   a. ________________________ are like _______________________ because both

   ____

   b. ...the musicians belabored their instruments like ________________________

4. ...the coming to his house of a bit of hopeful young life was like the lighting of a fire on a cold hearth. (page 25)

   _________________________ is like _________________________ because both

   ____

Name______________________________

b. ...the coming to his house of a bit of hopeful young life was like ___________

____

5. ...His wonder and his laughter ran together like spring rills in a thaw. (page 34)

a. ______________________ are like ______________________ because both

____

b. ...His wonder and his laughter ran together like ______________________

____

6. ...The motions of her mind were as incalculable as the flit of a bird in the branches. (page 35)

a. ______________________ are like ______________________ because both

____

b. The motions of her mind were as incalculable as ______________________

____

7. Here and there a farmhouse stood...mute and cold as a gravestone. (page 37)

a. ______________________ is like ______________________ because both

____

b. Here and there a farmhouse stood, mute and cold as ____________________

Name________________________________

Ethan Frome
Activity #15: **Critical Thinking**
Use With Video
Note: two-page activity

Directions: Watch the movie version of *Ethan Frome* by American Playhouse Theatrical Films (1992). Write a review of the movie. Include a comparison of the movie and the book. What changes were made to the story? What scenes or characters were added, deleted, condensed, changed? Why do you suppose the changes were made? Did the changes enhance the quality of the story or detract from it?

Use this framework to take notes on the book and the movie. The framework is designed to help you organize your ideas before writing the review.

The title of the film is ____________________. It was made in ____________________, stars

____________________________________ and was directed by ___________________________.

What I Liked About the Film	**What I Disliked**

(e.g., music, particular actor's acting, costuming, etc.)

Name______________________________

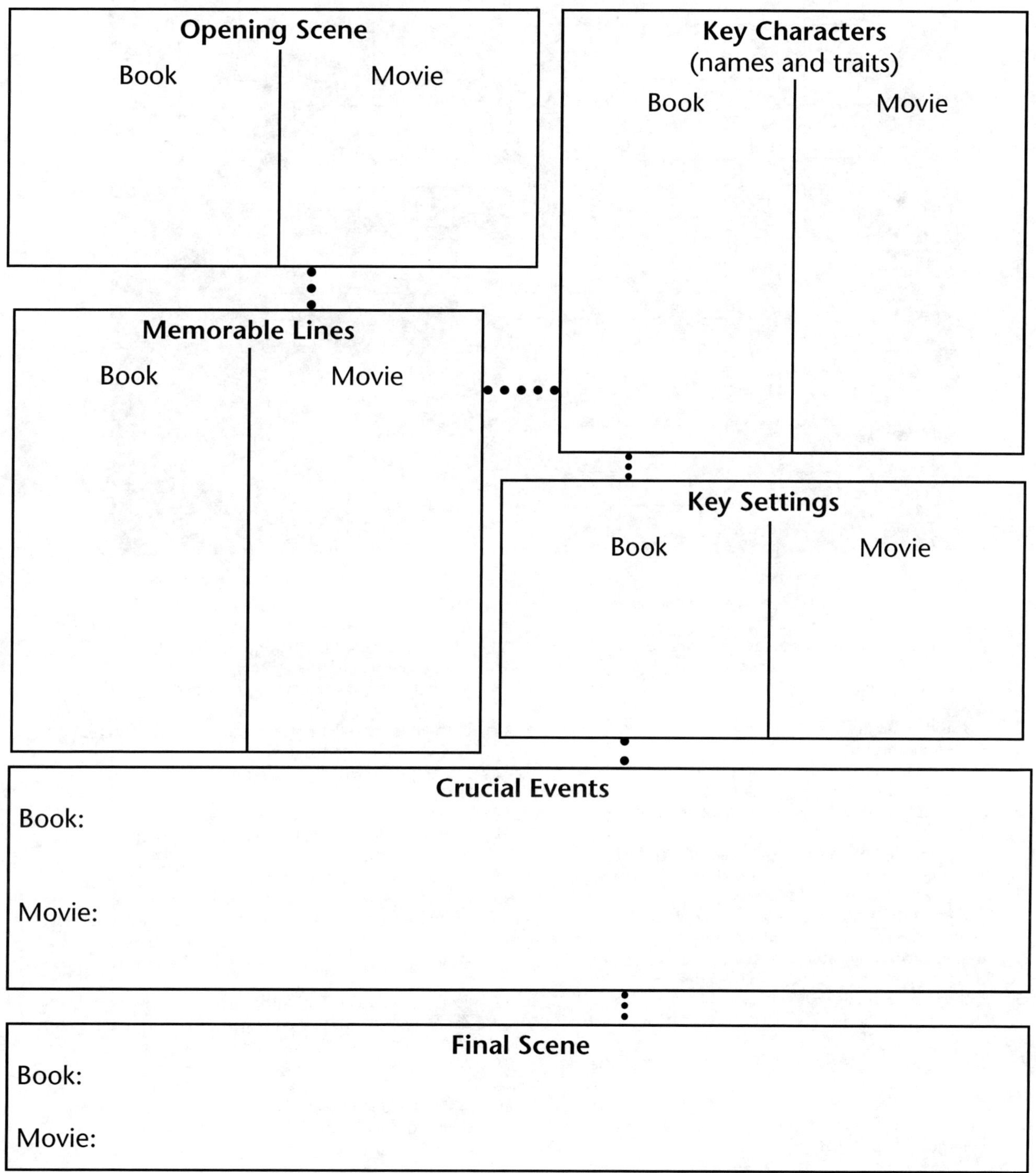
Opening Scene
Book
Movie
Key Characters
(names and traits)
Book
Movie
Memorable Lines
Book
Movie
Key Settings
Book
Movie
Crucial Events
Book:
Movie:
Final Scene
Book:
Movie:

Name________________________________

ACROSS

2. This friend of Mattie's married Ned and was later widowed.
4. At the dance, Mattie wore a cherry-colored one.
5. Mattie and Ethan rode one twice.
7. ___Gow told the narrator about Ethan's wreck.
9. what the sled hit
12. This story is set in a New ____ village.
14. Mattie tore this up.
16. Ethan and Mattie left home in this.
17. Ethan once found one Mattie had lost.
20. Mattie's father married into a family that ran this kind of business.
21. This caused the narrator to stay overnight at Ethan's.
22. Zeena never showed any ___ of Mattie.
29. Ethan feared Mattie would do this.
30. Because of these, Zeena needed a new girl.
32. He once planned to leave Starkfield.
33. Ethan looked in two stores for this.
34. Ethan thought of going here with Mattie.
35. Mattie was from this state.
37. Ethan's mother and Zeena both stopped doing much of this.
39. Mattie's relatives were angry that her father took their ___.
41. This Eady flirted with Mattie.
42. Ethan once paid $5 for this item, which Zeena wore when going out.

DOWN

1. She helped nurse Ethan's mother.
3. Ethan helped Mattie move this.
4. Zeena tried to keep Ethan home to fix this.
6. Mattie was a daughter of Zeena's _____.
8. She was ill herself when she came to Starkfield.
10. His picture was in Ethan's little room.
11. Both Ethan and the narrator had visited this state.
13. Edith _____ wrote this novel.
15. Mattie put a red one in her hair the night Zeena went away.
18. Ethan had left this state only once.
19. Zeena told Mattie to put pickles in the bottle that had held this.
23. The narrator was one.
24. Mattie enjoyed hearing Ethan talk about these.
25. As he stood on this, the narrator had a vision of Ethan's life.
26. Walking by these, Ethan fantasized about lying beside Mattie.
27. Ethan saw him kissing Ruth.
28. Zeena noticed that Ethan began to do this more often.
31. Ethan earned little from his poor farm and _____.
36. Zeena was furious that this dish was broken.
38. Mattie left home with $50 earned by selling this.
40. Ethan decided to wait for one of these before going sledding with Mattie.

Name________________________________

Ethan Frome
Comprehension Quiz • Level 1
Chapters 1-4

Directions: Mark each statement T for True or F for False.

___ 1. The narrator is an engineer who met Ethan Frome while working on a job near Starkfield.

___ 2. The narrator spent one winter as Ethan Frome's lodger.

___ 3. Harmon Gow said that Frome had been in a smash-up two years ago.

___ 4. Harmon Gow said that Frome's parents had been wealthy, but that Frome had lost the family fortune.

___ 5. Like the narrator, Ethan Frome had been to Florida.

___ 6. Ethan's wife Zeena was preoccupied with her health.

___ 7. Zeena had sent for Mattie because she felt sorry for her orphaned cousin.

___ 8. Ethan enjoyed attending the village dances with Mattie.

___ 9. Ethan was jealous when Mattie danced with Denis Eady.

___ 10. Zeena didn't complain about Mattie's housekeeping, for fear that Mattie would leave.

___ 11. Ethan and Mattie kissed before Zeena opened the door.

___ 12. Zeena made a surprise trip to Bettsbridge to buy a hat.

___ 13. When Zeena left, Ethan and Mattie spent the day sledding.

___ 14. Mattie accidentally dropped Zeena's pickle dish.

___ 15. Ethan planned to glue the dish and replace it without telling Zeena.

Matching: Match each cause with its effect.

Cause

___ 16. Ethan needed money.

___ 17. Ethan was in a smash-up.

___ 18. Mattie was sickly.

___ 19. Zeena decided to try a new doctor.

___ 20. Ethan's mother fell ill.

Effect

a. Ethan limped

b. Ethan sold his horse

c. Mattie and Ethan ate supper together, alone

d. Ethan drove the narrator to the train station for a week

e. Ethan used a wheel-chair

f. Ethan helped do housework when Zeena wasn't watching

g. Zeena came to the Frome farm

Name______________________________

Ethan Frome
Comprehension Quiz • Level 2
Chapters 1-4

Directions: Fill in each blank with a word or phrase that makes the statement true.

The narrator of the novel is a(n) 1.____________ who had been sent to work in Corbury Junction, 2.___________ (state) several years before. While staying in nearby 3.________________ at the home of Mrs. Ned Hale, he had met Ethan Frome and became interested in the man's life. According to the narrator's "vision" of Ethan Frome's story, Ethan's wife, Zeena, was a sour, sickly woman who was constantly preoccupied with her 4.____________ problems. Seeking help with the housework, she had sent for a poor relative, Mattie Silver. Ethan had taken to the vivacious young Mattie from the start, and for a period of 5.___________ he enjoyed her company—especially the nights when he got to walk her back from 6.____________ and other amusements at the village. On one such night, he noticed young 7.______________ flirting with Mattie, and grew jealous, but was reassured by Mattie's insistence that she did not want to leave the farm. Zeena surprised them both by meeting them at the threshold that night, announcing grumpily that she hadn't gone to bed as usual because she was 8.________________ __________________. Zeena did not seem jealous of Ethan's attentions to Mattie, she had begun to complain increasingly about Mattie's 9.______________, and Ethan grew uneasy. The next day Zeena made the surprise announcement that she was taking a trip to Bettsbridge to 10.________________. That night, Mattie put a 11.__________ in her hair and laid the table carefully for Ethan and herself. Their quiet enjoyment of the meal was marred by 12.________________, who knocked over Zeena's special 13.______________________. Ethan put the broken pieces on a high shelf and decided to solve the problem by 14.______________________.

Short Answer: Answer each question in a complete sentence. (Use the back of your paper.)

15. According to Harmon Gow, when—and how—did Ethan From become disabled?
16. Harmon Gow said that Ethan had had more than his share of sickness and trouble. What details did Gow supply to support his statement?
17. According to the narrator, how did the other people treat Ethan when he came in to town—and why?
18. According to Harmon Gow, why didn't Ethan Frome leave town like "most of the smart ones"?
19. How did Mrs. Ned Hale make the narrator even more curious about Ethan Frome?
20. How did the narrator end up spending the night at Ethan Frome's? What events led up to Frome's invitation?

Name________________________________

Identification: FInd a character in the box who matches the description on the left. Write the letter of the character next to the matching number. Each character is to be used only once.

A. Ethan Frome
B. Zeena
C. Mattie Silver
D. Ruth Varnum
E. Ned Hale
F. Denis Eady
G. Harmon Gow
H. Ethan's mother
I. Ethan's father
J. Jotham Powell

___ 1. the daughter of Zeena's cousin who came to the farm as her aid

___ 2. the part-time man who helped Ethan with the wood and drove Zeena home from the station

___ 3. Ethan's wife

___ 4. the young man who flirted with Mattie at the dance and went on to become a wealthy grocer

___ 5. This person's illness caused Ethan to be called away from his studies, back to the farm.

___ 6. the man who told the narrator as much of Ethan's story as his mental capacity allowed

___ 7. His limp was caused by a sled smash-up.

___ 8. the young man who married Ruth Varnum

___ 9. Zeena took care of her until she died.

___ 10. a close friend of Mattie's who later took in the narrator as a lodger

Multiple Choice: To the left of each item number, write the number of the BEST response.

___ 11. The narrator met Ethan while
- A. they were both growing up in Starkfield
- B. the narrator was working in Massachusetts
- C. Ethan was working in Florida
- D. Ethan was studying to be an engineer

___ 12. Which of the following did NOT stir up the narrator's interest in Ethan Frome?
- A. Ethan's limp
- B. Mrs. Hale's reluctance to talk about Ethan
- C. Harmon Gow's reluctance to talk about Ethan
- D. Ethan's grave expression

___ 13. Most of the details the narrator provides about Ethan's life are supplied by
A. Harmon Gow
B. the narrator's imagination
C. Ethan Frome
D. Mrs. Hale

___ 14. Zeena's reasons for taking Mattie in are most similar to the reasons
A. a godmother adopts an orphaned godchild
B. a foster mother takes in a foster child
C. a stroke victim hires a housekeeper
D. a parent hires a math tutor for her child

___ 15. The main reason Ethan married Zeena was that he
A. thought he was in love with her
B. felt sorry for her
C. thought she could finance his career
D. felt lonely the winter his mother died

___ 16. Like the narrator, Ethan at one time studied
A. botany
B. medicine
C. engineering
D. astronomy

___ 17. When Denis offered Mattie a ride home, she
A. accepted and made Ethan jealous
B. ran away laughing and walked home with Ethan
C. angrily told him to leave her alone
D. told him she was waiting for a ride with Ethan

___ 18. After the dance, Ethan was surprised by Zeena's appearance in the doorway because she
A. usually went to bed right after supper
B. had told him she would be at the doctor's
C. looked happier than usual to see him
D. made no attempt to hide her jealousy of Mattie

___ 19. Ethan told Zeena that he had to collect some money because
A. it was true
B. he didn't want her to worry about their debts
C. he wanted an excuse not to drive her
D. he didn't want her to know he planned to run off

___ 20. Mattie and Ethan were left alone together when Zeena
A. went into town for a new bonnet
B. went to the post office to pick up a package
C. went to take a mincemeat pie to a sick neighbor
D. went on a trip to see a new doctor

___ 21. After Ethan and Zeena were married
A. Ethan wanted to leave Starkfield for a bigger city, but Zeena was unwilling to go
B. Zeena wanted to leave Starkfield for a bigger city, but Ethan was unwilling to go
C. both Ethan and Zeena wanted to leave Starkfield, but Ethan's father would not hear of their going
D. Zeena wanted to leave Starkfield for a smaller town, but Ethan was unwilling to go

___ 22. At dinner with Ethan, Mattie was horrified when the cat broke Zeena's
A. flower vase
B. pickle dish
C. teapot
D. match-safe

___ 23. Alone together after dinner, Mattie and Ethan
A. sang at the piano
B. played cards
C. kissed
D. talked by the fire

___ 24. When Zeena went away, Ethan spent most of the day
A. sledding with Mattie
B. plowing his fields
C. hauling lumber with Jotham
D. walking with Mattie

___ 25. Ethan went to two stores looking for
A. a locket for Mattie
B. a science book
C. glue for a repair
D. a red hair ribbon for Mattie

___ 26. Zeena told Ethan that the new doctor had told her she
A. needed an operation
B. had nothing wrong with her
C. was dying
D. had complications

___ 27. Zeena claimed that she needed to hire another girl because
A. Ethan was paying too much attention to Mattie
B. Mattie had announced her intention to marry
C. Mattie had been stealing things
D. the doctor didn't want Zeena to do any housework

___ 28. When Ethan was called back to the farm by his father's illness, his mother gave him
A. a small room of his own
B. the family Bible
C. a photograph of his father
D. a pickle dish

___ 29. Which is NOT one of the reasons Ethan decided he couldn't run away with Mattie?
A. Zeena would have trouble keeping the farm going.
B. Finding a buyer for the farm would be difficult.
C. Ethan still loved Zeena in his way.
D. Ethan didn't have enough money to take Mattie West.

___ 30. Ethan wrote a letter in which he
A. blamed Zeena for the unhappy state of their marriage
B. told Zeena why he was committing suicide
C. told Zeena that he was going West
D. told Mattie that he couldn't leave his wife

___ 31. What tone of voice do you think Zeena used when she mentioned the huckabuck towels to Mattie before Mattie's departure?
A. accusing
B. apologetic
C. sorrowful
D. playful

___ 32. Zeena told Ethan to let Jotham drive Mattie to the station so that Ethan could
A. stay home and glue her pickle dish
B. stay home and fix the stove
C. go to Ned Hale's to pick up the payment
D. go to town to pick up her medicine

___ 33. When the time came for Mattie to leave the house, Zeena
A. threw Mattie's hair ribbon out the door
B. stiffly wished her luck
C. slammed the door on her
D. had gone upstairs without saying good-bye

___ 34. Ethan and Mattie's sled hit the tree because
A. Ethan was unable to see it without moonlight
B. Ethan wasn't used to steering this sled
C. they planned to die together
D. Mattie grabbed Ethan's arm at the last moment

___ 35. Twenty-four years after the accident
A. Mattie was paralyzed, but still had a "sweet nature"
B. Ethan decided to try to get an engineering job
C. Ethan was still planning to move West
D. Ethan, Mattie, and Zeena lived together

Name________________________________

Written Response

I. Analysis

Directions: Select A or B and indicate the letter of the question you decide to answer. Answer in one well-organized paragraph.

A. Compare and contrast Mattie and Zeena at the end of the story. Include at least two similarities and one difference.

B. Describe the setting of this story. Include the time, the place, and the types of people in that setting.

II. Critical and Creative Thinking

Directions: Select C or D

C. Has Wharton done a good job of making Ethan Frome a believable character? Describe your impressions of Ethan Frome and explain why he does or does not seem real to you.

D. Suppose Ethan had found a way to go West with Mattie. Do you think things would have worked out? Pretend that you are Mattie and write a letter to your friend Ruth, a year after you leave Starkfield.

Name_______________________________

Identification: Explain who each character is and briefly describe his or her significance in the novel.

1. Ethan Frome
2. Zeena
3. Mattie Silver
4. Ruth Varnum
5. Ned Hale
6. Denis Eady
7. Harmon Gow
8. Ethan's mother
9. Ethan's father
10. Jotham Powell

Short Answer: Answer each question in one or two complete sentences.

1. How did the narrator meet Ethan?
2. Why was the narrator interested in Ethan?
3. How did the narrator learn details about Ethan's life?
4. Why did Zeena take Mattie into her home?
5. Why did Ethan marry Zeena?

Name_______________________________

6. How was the narrator like Ethan?

7. What did Denis Eady and Mattie think of each other?

8. Why did Ethan lie about going to collect money from Mr. Hale?

9. How did Mattie and Zeena end up alone together in the house overnight?

10. Why didn't Ethan leave Starkfield when he and Zeena were newlyweds?

11. How did Zeena's pickle dish get broken and how did she react?

12. According to Zeena, why was it necessary to get rid of Mattie and hire another servant?

13. How were Ethan's studies interrupted when he was young?

14. Why did Ethan decide he couldn't run away with Mattie?

15. What was in the letter that Ethan wrote?

16. How did Zeena try to keep Ethan from driving Mattie to the station? Why?

17. Why did Mattie and Ethan take the sled down the hill the first time?

18. Why did Mattie and Ethan take the sled down the hill the second time?

19. What happened in the days right after the accident? How do you know?

20. What is Ethan's home life like, 24 years after the accident? How do you know?

Name________________________________

Essay

I. Analysis
Directions: Select A or B and indicate the letter of the question you decide to answer.

A. Describe the framework structure (story within a story) of *Ethan Frome.*

B. Why does Mrs. Hale say that if Mattie had died, Ethan might have lived?

II. Critical/Creative Thinking
Directions: Select C or D and indicate the letter of the question you decide to answer.

C. You are Ethan. Often you go into your private "study" to write in your journal. Write four entries—the day Mattie comes into your home, the day you learn that Zeena plans to send Mattie away, a week after the accident, five years after the accident.

D. You are Zeena. Write an interior monologue that reveals your thoughts after the argument you have with Ethan about sending Mattie away.

Answer Key

Activity #1: Students should be encouraged to discuss and support their answers to this and other open-ended activities for which there are no right or wrong answers.

Study Questions
Introductory Comments (pages 3-19)

1. Ethan has a scar on his face, limps, and looks depressed.
2. He was in a "smash-up."
3. According to Harmon Gow, Ethan was responsible for caring for his father, then his mother, then his wife. Then came the smash-up.
4. He is on an engineering job at a power-house in a nearby town.
5. He hired Ethan to drive him to the train station to work each day, once Eady's horses got ill.
6. He had a job in Florida once.
7. He leaves it in Ethan's sleigh; Ethan reads it, expresses an interest in it, accepts it on loan.
8. There is a heavy snowstorm going on.

Chapter 1

1. He was called home to work the farm after his father died.
2. He has come to take Mattie home from a dance.
3. Eady, the son of a grocer, dances and flirts with Mattie and offers her a ride.
4. A distant relative of Zeena's, she has come as Zeena's aide.
5. He enjoys the fact that he can tell her about the stars, rocks, etc., and feel that she listens and appreciates.
6. She is critical of Mattie's housekeeping.
7. The doctor has apparently said that Zeena has complications and must take it easier; Zeena implies that she still has to do too much because of Mattie's incompetence.
8. She is probably getting in a dig about the fact that he shows more concern for his appearance since Mattie's arrival.

Chapter 2

1. Denis Eady offers Mattie a ride.
2. Mattie waits while he makes room for her next to him, then runs away.
3. Mattie mentions that Ned and Ruth nearly ran their sled into the elm.
4. She doesn't directly deny interest in Denis, but worries aloud that Zeena may be unhappy with her and acts distressed by the idea of leaving.
5. He tells Mattie that Ned isn't much good at steering, but he—Ethan—could take Mattie down on the sled all right.
6. Often he feels depressed by the thought that he will live on the farm until he joins the other corpses; tonight he is happy at the thought that he will stay on the farm with Mattie and she will one day lie near him in the graveyard.
7. The key is not under the mat where Zeena usually leaves it.
8. She says that she is up because she feels ill.

Chapter 3

1. Zeena is silent.
2. Mattie has become healthier, prettier.
3. He died after losing the savings of several relatives in a crooked scheme of some sort.
4. Zeena decided that her health dictated a need for someone to help her; Zeena knew that she would be able to find fault with Mattie without risk of losing her because the girl was penniless.
5. Zeena is going to Bettsbridge to see a new doctor.

6. Ethan is 28 and Zeena is 35.
7. He makes up a quick excuse so that he will not have to drive Zeena to the station.
8. He doesn't want her to think that there is extra money coming in, or she may spend it on her excursion.

Chapter 4

1. He had planned to move out of Starkfield to get an engineering job in a larger town.
2. She grew ill, developed mental problems, stopped talking, and died.
3. Zeena took over after she came to help nurse Ethan's mother, and Ethan was lonely after his mother died in the winter.
4. She didn't want to go where people would "look down on her."
5. She started complaining about her health, grew quiet.
6. Ethan knows that Zeena will remember that he had said there was extra money coming in.
7. Ethan is afraid that Denis Eady will have come to court Mattie and that Eady's horse will be in the barn.
8. Mattie puts out the dish to set the table specially and the cat knocks the dish to the floor.

Chapter 5

1. Ethan eats, Mattie sips tea, they talk about commonplace things like the weather, then sit by the fire while Mattie works on her sewing.
2. Ethan points out that they wouldn't be able to see on such a moonless night.
3. Ethan saw Ruth and Ned kissing.
4. She jumps from Zeena's chair after a mouse and starts the chair rocking.
5. Ethan kisses the fabric she is sewing.
6. She drags the cat bed toward the stove, and moves the plants away from the cold window.

Chapter 6

1. It is cold, sleeting, and icy.
2. He wants to buy glue so that he can fix the dish.
3. They end up hauling lumber all day.
4. He goes first to Eady's store, then to the widow Homan's.
5. By the time he gets home, Zeena is already there.
6. Zeena goes straight to her room without a word.
7. He has driven Zeena home and probably knows that she is in a particularly bad mood.
8. Mattie again sets the table and sits, alone, with Ethan.

Chapter 7

1. The new doctor has told Zeena that she has "complications."
2. Zeena says that the doctor has indicated that she needs more help than she is currently getting.
3. Zeena has hired the new girl without consulting Ethan, and he is concerned about the expense and about Mattie leaving.
4. Ethan has not collected any payment from Hale.
5. Mattie is Zeena's relative, not his.
6. She has no money and few skills.
7. Zeena indicates that Mattie's pie has given her heartburn.
8. She goes to look for stomach medicine and finds the pieces of the dish on the shelf.

Chapter 8

1. It is a small room behind the parlor, where he has put up bookshelves, a box-sofa, a picture of Lincoln, a calendar with poetic sayings.
2. "Don't trouble, Ethan."
3. The man left his wife and went West with the woman he loved.
4. He explains that he is leaving her, doesn't blame her, that she can sell the farm and mill and keep the money.

5. He sees the price of a ticket West and realizes he cannot afford the trip.
6. He realizes that he cannot desert her.
7. Zeena wants to know where a certain towel and match-safe are.
8. He has decided that he will ask Andrew Hale for a loan.

Chapter 9

1. Mattie had made the room cozier by putting a red and white quilt to her bed, a pretty pin cushion on her chest of drawers, a photograph of her mother over the dresser, some dyed grasses in the back.
2. He is angry that Mattie is lifting the trunk by herself.
3. She says that Ethan should stay and fix the stove for the new girl.
4. He wants to go by the spot where he and Mattie attended a picnic together.
5. She says that she will try to get a place in a store.
6. Mattie tears up the letter that Ethan had written to Zeena because she knows that there is no use in thinking of a life together.
7. At first, they want to experience the thrill together as they hold on to each other.
8. They want to die together when the sled hits the tree.

Narrator's Concluding Comments (pages 127-133)

1. She is small, gray-haired, wizened, paralyzed, and has witch-like eyes.
2. They gripe at each other constantly.
3. Zeena went to stay with Ethan and had Mattie brought to the farm to stay with them.
4. Mrs. Hale says that Zeena has "raised up" by the call to take care of Ethan and Mattie, and some of her strength came back.
5. Mattie has become sour, irritable.
6. Mrs. Hale feels that Ethan might have had more of a life without the responsibility.

Activity #2
1-beleaguered; 2-effrontery; 3-reticence; 4-inertia; 5-dormant; 6-plaintive; 7-querulously; 8-fatuity; 9-livery; 10-incisively

Activity #3
1-E; 2-A; 3-D; 4-E; 5-B; 6-B; 7-D; 8-C; 9-A; 10-D

Activity #4 (other acceptable answers in parentheses)
1-pauper; 2-compunction; 3-inexorable; 4-indolent (or ponderous); 5-ponderous; 6-ominous; 7-perfunctory; 8-stoicism (or affability); 9-ineffectual; 10-rupture; 11-irretrievable; 12-regaled; 13-antipathy; 14-derision (or recrimination); 15-irrationally

Activity #5
1-swarthy; 2-immobility; 3-ebullition; 4-avowal; 5-reflectively; 6-facetious; 7-discursively; 8-relic; 9-passively; 10-injunction; 11-subdue; 12-contemptuously; 13-niche; 14-opaque; 15-monotonous

Activity #6
Reasons to leave Zeena include: Zeena is hateful, spiteful; Mattie needs Ethan; Reasons to stay with Zeena include: Ethan's sense of loyalty to their marriage; Zeena would be left sick, poor, alone; the community would censor Ethan.

Activity #7
Opinions will differ. Those who argue against the joint suicide may point out that Mattie and Ethan might have had a life together somewhere else. Those who argue for the suicide attempt might point out that Ethan and Mattie felt trapped, that this was their only way to stay together.

Activity #8
Essays might include these details: In her youth, Mattie was pretty, vibrant, considerate, upbeat, interested in Ethan, whereas Zeena was angry, self-concerned, hypochondriacal, sabotaging Ethan's happiness even when younger. As older women, both were unattractive, whiny, self-centered, taking from Ethan while giving little in return.

Activity #9
I. **Resonance:** Page references will vary. A. Through references to Mattie's red scarf, hair ribbon, red cheeks, red comes to symbolize vitality. B. Sledding down below Varnum's spruces stands for reckless danger. C. Ned and Ruth's kiss, mentioned several times, symbolizes the socially-approved and expressed love that is denied Ethan and Mattie. D. The numerous references to the threshold of the farmhouse emphasize the contrast between the world of possibility outside that door and the limitations of a life with Zeena. E. The snow emphasizes the stifling isolation of Starkfield. F. The train is the symbol for life outside of town. G. The name "Starkfield" suggests how bleak a place it is.
II. **Setting:** A. Mattie came to the farm 25 years before the narrator met Frome. Since the story was written in 1911 (which would be about the right year for the narrator's references to trolleys, etc.) this would indicate that Mattie's arrival was around 1885. B. The story takes place in Starkfield, a small town in western Massachusetts with a post office, a church, a grocery store, and a train station. Ethan wanted to live and work in a larger place with a more cosmopolitan atmosphere, but Zeena didn't want to live in a larger town where people might "look down on her." C. The story takes place in winter. Ethan is feeling isolated, and depressed; the snow literally isolates the town and makes it more bleak in winter. D. the trolley, rural delivery E. She has personalized her room with a picture of her mother, a pretty pin cushion, and dried flowers. She cares about pretty things. F. Ethan has put up bookshelves, a calendar of poetic sayings, and a picture of Lincoln. He cares about learning. G. Mattie had kept the house fairly bright. Now it is decrepit; the furniture is rough; the plates are chipped. It is old and feels as dead as Ethan does.
III. **Doppelganger:** A. Ethan sees Zeena's face superimposed on Mattie's when Mattie sits in Zeena's chair. B. Both are whiny, gray-haired, and shriveled. C. Both have studied engineering, worked in Florida. D. Perhaps she is showing what the narrator could have become, under different, restrictive social conditions—or what Ethan could have become under better circumstances.

Activity #10
Accounts will vary, but should include the basic facts a reporter would glean: Mattie and Ethan had been sledding on Corbury Road at sunset when their sled hit a tree, injuring both and paralyzing Mattie.

Activity #11
Sample translations: 1-There wasn't ever anybody but Ethan. First his father—then his mother—then his wife. 2-We're rather isolated now...but many people passed by before the railroad was extended through the Flats. 3-The doctor doesn't want me to be left without anyone to help me. 4-Sometimes I can see that she isn't satisfied with me, and yet I don't know why. 5-Of all my possessions, you took the one thing that I cared most about. 6-Oh, Matt, I thought we would die.

Activity #12
The letters will vary. Zeena would probably complain about her husband's attentions to her cousin, her cousin's incompetence, and her health problems, which would be extensive. Gabby might advise her to get the girl out of her house and concentrate on eating well and getting exercise.

Activity #13
Students should be given time to do pre- and post-writing activities together.

Activity #14 (Student similes in part b will vary.)

1. Ethan's gait is like that of a prisoner who is shackled; both jerk and both are confined.
2. Ethan's profile is like a hero's statue; both are cold, passionless, suggestive of courage.
3. The musicians are like horseback riders; both put a lot of energy into urging on (their horse/instrument).
4. Mattie's arrival was like lighting a fire; both bring warmth.
5. His wonder and laughter are like streams in a thaw; both arise, gurgling and alive, after a period of cold, frozen silence.
6. Her thoughts are like a bird's movements; both are erratic and hard to predict.
7. Each farmhouse is like a gravestone; both are silent and cold.

Activity #15
Graphics and reviews will vary. Students might mention these differences: While both the film and the book use a narrator and a story-within-the-story, the narrator in the book is an engineer (not a minister), Ethan and Mattie are more hesitant to kiss and otherwise express their attraction, Ethan's mother is mentioned only briefly, and the accident is clearly the result of a suicide attempt.

Activity #16: Crossword Puzzle

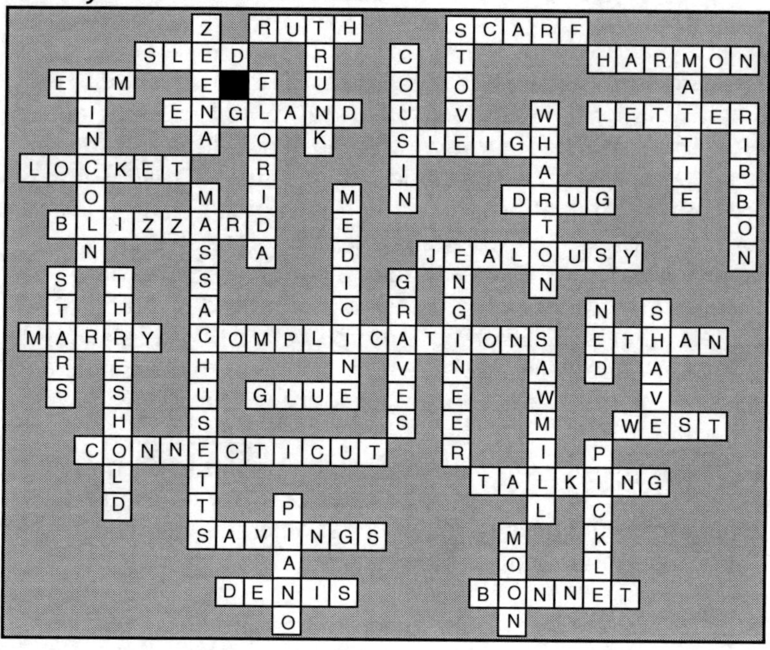

Comprehension Quiz, Level 1
True-False: 1-T; 2-F; 3-F; 4-F; 5-T; 6-T; 7-F; 8-F; 9-T; 10-F; 11-F; 12-F; 13-F; 14-F; 15-T
Matching: 16-d; 17-a; 18-f; 19-c; 20-g

Comprehension Quiz, Level 2
Sentence Completion:
1-engineer; 2-Massachusetts; 3-Starkfield; 4-health; 5-one year; 6-dances; 7-Denis Eady; 8-feeling too ill to sleep; 9-housekeeping; 10-see a new doctor; 11-red ribbon; 12-Zeena's cat; 13-pickle dish; 14-gluing the pieces the next morning and then looking for a replacement.
Short Answer: 15. Ethan was in a smash-up 24 years earlier. 16. Gow mentioned that in addition to the smash-up, Ethan Frome had taken care of his sick parents, then his wife. 17. Others spoke to him rarely, as he didn't seem desirous of conversation. 18. He was held back by the sickness of his parents, his wife, and then by the smash-up. 19. Her hesitance about discussing Ethan piqued the narrator's curiosity still more. 20. Ethan had been driving him to and from the train station. A blizzard made travel difficult.

Novel Test, Level 1
Identification: 1-C; 2-J; 3-B; 4-F; 5-I; 6-G; 7-A; 8-E; 9-H; 10-D
Multiple Choice: 11-B; 12-C; 13-B; 14-C; 15-D; 16-C; 17-B; 18-A; 19-C; 20-D; 21-A; 22-B; 23-D; 24-C; 25-C; 26-D; 27-D; 28-A; 29-C; 30-C; 31-A; 32-B; 33-D; 34-C; 35-D
Written Response (Details that should be found in student answers:)

I. A. Both are gray-haired, wrinkled, and crotchety; Zeena is able to walk while Mattie is confined to the chair.
B. The main story takes place in Starkfield, Massachusetts—a small, isolated town—during the winter 24 years before the frame story. Everyone knows everyone else; many like to gossip.

II. C. The narrator's description of Ethan as a young man and an older one present someone who has been tormented by his love for someone he cannot have, someone whose dreams have been extinguished by a vindictive wife and a smothering social environment.
D. Mattie would probably describe her home, the job Ethan has found, Ethan's happiness (or restlessness).

Novel Test, Level 2
Identification

1. Ethan Frome is the main character of the story, a man who was trapped by his marriage and whose love for his wife's cousin could never be actualized.
2. Zeena is Ethan's hypochondriacal, complaining wife, a woman who stifled her husband.
3. Mattie Silver is Zeena's relative, a vibrant young woman who comes to help Zeena and falls in love with Ethan.
4. Ruth Varnum is a good friend of Mattie's who marries Ned and later, as a widow, houses the narrator and speaks to him about the sledding accident and its aftermath.
5. Ned Hale is the young man who marries Ruth Varnum, the son of a warm-hearted friend of Ethan's.
6. Denis Eady, the son of a grocer, flirts with Mattie and years later becomes a prosperous grocer.
7. Harmon Gow, a former stage driver, supplies the narrator with details about Ethan's past.
8. Ethan's mother grew physically ill, then quiet and paranoid before she died, in his care.
9. Ethan's father died, forcing Ethan to leave school and assume responsibility for the farm.
10. Powell was a hired man who worked sometimes with Ethan, and drove Zeena the day she went to see a new doctor.

Short Answer

1. The narrator was working at a powerhouse in a nearby town when a carpenters' strike forced him to stay the winter in Starkfield. The narrator noticed Ethan picking up his mail, and met him when he asked if Ethan would drive him back and forth to the train.
2. The narrator was intrigued by Ethan's appearance—his limp, his gloom—by what he had heard about a tragic "smash-up"—and by certain similarities in their backgrounds (both engineers, both having worked in Florida).
3. Ethan learned some details from Harmon Gow and others, and imagined the rest.
4. Zeena was sickly and wanted someone to help her with her housework. Since Mattie was a penniless, orphaned relative, she seemed the likely candidate.
5. Zeena had taken care of his mother and competently taken over the household. When his mother died, he was lonely and marrying Zeena seemed to make sense.
6. Like Ethan, the narrator was an engineer and had worked in Florida.
7. Eady was interested in Mattie, and she danced with him, but didn't encourage him much and seemed to find the idea of marriage to him laughable.
8. Ethan wanted an excuse not to have to drive Zeena to the train, so invented this errand.
9. Zeena decided to go to Bettsbridge to see a new doctor.
10. He found that Zeena was resistant to moving to a larger town where people would "look down on her." Also, there were no buyers for the farm and sawmill.

11. When Zeena left, Mattie got down the pickle dish to set a special table for Ethan, and the cat knocked the dish off the table. Mattie was horrified at the thought of how angry Zeena would be.
12. Zeena said that the doctor didn't want her to have to work around the house and Zeena implied that Mattie did not do enough.
13. He had to return to the farm when his father died, and then his mother grew ill.
14. He didn't have the money for the trip and he couldn't bear to think of deserting Zeena—sick, with only the small amount that she would get from sale of the farm.
15. Ethan wrote to Zeena that he was leaving her to go out West, that he didn't blame her, and that she could have the money from the sale of the farm and sawmill.
16. Zeena ordered Ethan to stay and fix the stove—probably because she wanted to make a good impression on the new girl, and also because she didn't want Ethan alone with Mattie.
17. The first time, they wanted the thrill and the closeness.
18. The second time, they wanted to go to their deaths together.
19. Zeena went to be with Ethan and ordered that Mattie, who nearly died, be taken to their home.
20. Ethan's home life is bleak and miserable, with Zeena and Mattie constantly complaining. The narrator tells what he sees when he enters the farmhouse and Mrs. Hale tells how unhappy the household has been since the accident.

Essay

I. A. The narrator describes what Ethan is like 24 years after the smash-up, then imagines what life was like for him during the days leading up to the accident.

B. If she had died, he could have loved her memory. As it is, she has become as much of a shrew as Zeena, and his hopes for a different life have been completely squelched by his responsibility to the two women.

II. C. The entries should reflect events and emotions from the story—Ethan's initial attraction to Mattie, his anger about Zeena's sending her away, his initial despair when he learns that she is paralyzed, his sense of powerlessness years later.

D. The monologue should reveal her anger toward Ethan, who is obviously infatuated with Mattie, her jealousy of Mattie, and her self-absorption and health concerns.